Poems That Lose

Poems That Lose

Akif Kichloo

First edition published globally by
Read Out Loud Publishing LLP in 2017.

ISBN: 0997937645
ISBN-13: 9780997937640

©Akif Kichloo, All Rights Reserved.

Akif asserts the moral right to be identified as the author of this work.

All Rights Reserved. No part of this publication may be reproduced, stored in a retrieval form, or transmitted, in an form or by any means, electronic, mechanical, photocopying, recording or otherwise without the prior permission of the publishers.

Cover design by Adnan Khateeb
Cover art by Surbhi Pathania

(www.akifkichloo.com)

To the thinkers (with their protrusions and depressions).

CONTENTS

Introduction   Pg 11

Poems   Pg 15

About The Author   Pg 101

What if the poem loses?
What if it never tastes victory like the
intent it was written with?

INTRODUCTION

I am an artless poet.
My metaphors come from an artless place.

My heart doesn't open like a blooming
flower *(common metaphor)*
but breaks like a beer bottle on a pavement
instead *(artless fact)*.
I cannot, anymore, for the life of me, keep talking
about beauty and richness and extravagant sunsets,
or the wholeness of my existence.
This is my time to talk
about
unkempt hair
and cigarettes after sex,
about
the inherent violence in our existence
and the ruins of love living(dying)
in sewers, drinking sewer-water.

I am an artless poet.
From today, until I "make it"
my metaphors shall come from the
artless place I belong.

Akif Kichloo

Trigger Warning

This book contains some poems on subjects of depression, suicide, and sexual assault.

Akif Kichloo

Poems That Lose

Poems

The lesson, dear human:
All loving is not benign.

I have a body too young
and a mind full of years.
Everything in me has
witnessed its own ending.
I have lived through nightmares
and died in blissful dreams.
What all that's left in me
either eats me from within
or melts me from without,
and that is where my
humility takes form.

—The curse

Poems That Lose

No disease is gentle;
every affliction an equal a calamity.

I—
a medicine man;

Learned enough,
Able enough
to cure everything,

Still know not how—

to cure this sclerosis of souls.

— A pandemic I am determined to cure

Akif Kichloo

It's summer,
the roads have melted,
the tar on them sticky,
the asphalt drained away
into the gutters no one knows about;

nothing is safe from the looming rain my
grandmother feels in her bones.

My feet wear concrete boots as I walk;
too heavy to take these steps,
but still I take one at a time
wishing I get to *life* before they do.

The air is humid;
it steals breaths from my lungs
and leaves me gasping for
something more.
Something I can hold
inside me like more than just a breath.

I have seen enough,
been through way more
than my fair share;
Summers were never meant to
feel this heavy.
My childhood pictures
remind me of lighter days.

—Snapshot of the present moment

Poems That Lose

I exist in two states on my lover's bed.
First, a toddler in love.
I mumble words when I am scared;
my voice squeaky,
my touch infantile.
I want my lover to caress me like a
mother cares for her child.

Then, out of nowhere
that force hits me
and I turn into a grown man;
my voice—a much lower octave,
often heaving through my chest.

A man's aroused body is better than his aroused mind:
It is predisposed to growing with love.

And next, all the to and fro,
the back and forth;
the mindful mindless motion of procreation—
until climax.

The man stays with me for a while after,
but then— the post-coital cuddling— again—
as incestious as ever.

— *The dichotomy of men*

At 3. a.m., I am a euphoric do-it-all.
I would conquer the world if only
the battles happened at 3. a.m.

—*Mania*

Poems That Lose

I look at my father—
though a harsh man,
I wonder what he would have been like
when he was my age.

I think
crude,
unromantic,
a manly man.
You know the ones who are not in
touch with their feminine side.

But once I found a love poem
hand written inside one of his old books
from medical school.
It talked about a man's wish
to walk with his lover,
hand in hand
outside in the rain.

It is hard to imagine my father in love.

Maybe he loved that woman in the poem
so much,
he used up all his love?

—*A poem from the teenage years*

Once when I was six years old,
I confused my father for a stone.
This day, twenty-four years later I
understand exactly the reason why.

—*Indifference comes easy with age/ Like father like son*

Poems That Lose

That window which connects you
to the agony of other people;
that's your soul.
Close that window and you are soulless.
And a soulless man is vestigial.
He hears but cannot listen.
He sees but cannot notice.

And everyone knows:
when eyes and ears become jobless,

We look for excuses.
We hear angels and devils speak.
We confabulate.
We make up gods
and lick their feet.

—*Superstitions*

Triggers

(i) I stare at the wall and it stares back at me.
(No dandelion fields for me today; only staircases I want to trip from.)

(ii) I saved a poem for this day.
The sky won't cry any more. It has been dry like the eyes with no love left in them.
(Couples have to grow old.)

(iii) I am big and only infants are allowed to be held by their fathers as they weep. Who knows if they see what most of us don't. Who knows if they are watching the face of their father freeze cold and unrelenting, ("Son, you have grown up now" he says). I have nothing cute to tell him except it is a matter of life and death now. I have had black eyes ever since I was born, and I have been watching my father the same way. Light. Flowers on his skin. Loss on his forehead. Helpless hands always ready to give but not give up.

(iv) Trigger: There is silence here. He is not here anymore.
She tells me, no one loves you like I do and I think she is right.
My depression has been telling me the same.
(Mothers have a way with words.)

(v) Silence interrupted: I am safe for a while.
God please take me before you take him. I am not good with dealing with loss.

Trigger: Nightmares. He is leaving! He is leaving!
(I am wide awake. The journal by my bed stares cold. "Don't write. Call your dad.")

(vi) Blood disappears under my skin. My nails don't grow at all. All my life I have fought with god. How dare you? How dare you?
(Anxiety is born sometimes in innocence too.)

(People die in mysterious ways. Will my father know if I did too. And if he knows, will he hold me like he did when I was small?)

(vii) I will not eat tonight. I will not eat tonight. I will *NOT* eat tonight. "Maybe just a bowl?"

(viii) There are no sharp corners left in my body. I do not know how to harm others anymore.
(Like father like son.)

The wall is crumbling. The room is shrinking. My claustrophobia heavy on my chest.
(I sleep with the lights on.)

(ix) She thinks she lies out of love. "Mother, you don't lie out of love. No one ever lies out of love."

(x) Trigger: I am alone. The water is rising. I am neck deep in my own mess.

Trigger: I am dying. I am dying. I am dying.
Someone, please call my dad.

My heart is filled with
something terrible;
Some form of sickness I fail to understand.
I don't know if it's my love for you
or the pain of your absence.
All I know is
that I am tetanized;
Moved—
to the point of paralysis.

—The dilemma

Poems That Lose

There is
nothing here
but this
haunting presence
of your absence.
I have been finally
left alone by everything
but solitude.
Tonight seems like
a perfect night
to mourn

    you.

—*tum incipit vita nova (then begins a new life)*

—*I loved you, now I shall mourn*

How many laugh lines there
must be on my face
that can be attributed to you.
I carry you with me—
like this—
not just in memories
but in tangible form.

And with age,
as old fires cool,
these lines will deepen
and I guess this is how we will
grow old together now.

—*Without you*

Poems That Lose

"You have a big heart. I think sadness arrived early in your life."

—The empathic

Akif Kichloo

I have been through tragedy
and one day I intend to remember it.
Until then, can I look at flowers
and play pretend that nothing horrible
ever happened to me?

There is this filthy tapestry to assault;
moral, sexual, or whatever kind—
always binding the one harassed
to their perpetrator.

Some call people like me "victims"
and I ask them "victims" of what?

The tap of my memory is turned off,
but an occasional drop flows through every
now and then:
Sometimes in the form of horrifying flashbacks,
and sometimes in the form of gratifying violent sex.

— The rape fantasy/bondage

Poems That Lose

Then she says, "Meeting new people is such a big burden for me."
"One hand shake, a couple of drinks, and just like that— their story is not theirs anymore."
"As if a truck-full of concrete, unloaded off their chest and
straight into mine."
"The cruelty in the act of looking someone in the eye, you know,"
"I don't have words to describe it."

"I understand," I hear my lips move,
"One look into their eyes and then weeks of nothing but sleepless nights, wondering, how that much sadness could ever fit inside such small human beings."

—*All of us are bottomless wells of memories
 from our glory days*

—*A conversation about the times introversion
 becomes a necessity*

I wake up in a trans,
It is a warm summer day.
My neck is sweaty
and last night's light hasn't left my mind.
Do you know the bodies of prophets
sweated just like yours did last night?
And there is nothing special about that,
unless it's your sweat
and I sweat with you
and my eyes see the sweat dripping
from your skin.
It is not pearly.
I won't call it diamonds.
Let's not give names to things
we think need uplifting.
Sweat doesn't need uplifting;
Woman's sweat and man's sweat—
let's not discriminate.
Calling a spade a spade is not a sin.
Calling a spade a mountain is delusional.
I saw you last night,
and we made love.
It was messy,
and we sweated a lot.
That's our unrosy romance
and it is what it is.

—It is what it is

Poems That Lose

The opposite of *grief* is not laughter or happiness or joy. It is *love*. It is *love*. It is *love*.

—*What we need to understand*

This coming and going of people,
Landing of airplanes and then their
abrupt taking off;
It feels like some sub-conscious state of delusion
we live with constantly in our heads.
As if we—as a whole race—can never
be innocent again.

—Airport observations

Poems That Lose

I fear the world,
sometimes for its quiet,
sometimes for its indecision,
sometimes for its lack of presence,
but never for its riots,
never for its resilience,
never for its strength.

When it stands up
for ruckus
or for cause,
there is this reassurance,
that we are here,
that we are thinking,
that we want the best
for us
for us
for us.

But what when it gets tired,
and decides to call quits?
Where will I go?

A Muslim name
without a Muslim god.
Who will come and save me then?
And if I don't need the saving,
who will come and send me on my way
to hell?

—With the rest of us.

People have taken Him hostage.
He is not around anymore.
I hear Him weep at times.
"Have mercy," He cries from behind the bars,
"Have mercy. Have mercy. Have mercy."

I, like many, turn the other way
and mind my own business.

I, like many, have learned my lessons from the words
of God.

— *2 Corinthians 9:6*
(The point is this: whoever sows sparingly will also
reap sparingly, and whoever sows bountifully will also
reap bountifully.)

Poems That Lose

If You have to punish me, like this, dear God,
for my strength,
harass me for my perseverance,
Then how do I give them back?
I do not want them.
I want neither this strength nor this perseverance.
Where do I go to find Your returns department?

— *Quran 2:286*
(Allah does not burden a soul beyond that it can bear)

—*When God says no backsies*

Akif Kichloo

What soil am I made of?
What color is my skin?
It turns red, and then brown, and then
black with the sun,
and how long do I hide
to stop it from changing its tint?

What questions do I ask?
How proud should I be of my shadow?
Do I run *or* embrace my being
in all these shapes, colors, and forms?

I feel like a shapeless man,
Opaque with blunders.
I show up everywhere I am not supposed to be;
omnipresent in my mistakes.

What name is my god?
And what name do I give myself
if I decide to wear a different god's uniform?

—*Who am I?*

Poems That Lose

The first time we tied each-other up,
in wild ecstasy, slapped each-other's faces,
and made a mess of the bedroom floor,
I remember the Friday sermon was going on
in the mosque beside my room.

It's as if yesterday,
I laid my spinning head on her peachy breasts;
both of us bruised and equally spent—

when the priest on the loudspeaker
                said,

"Women are only good for household chores."

To which her comeback was, "I hate these cheeky bastards in long beards."

—The venomous priest and the woman's roar

Akif Kichloo

Like obsequious barmaids
we try our best to lubricate God,
service Him with all our time.

For what?
Some twisted dream
of pomegranate breasted angels *(hoors)*,
rivers of wine we cannot get high on,
and a few beautiful looking butterflies?

If my God is supreme
What good am I to him?

What help do you think
He needs from me?

And what good does it do for me
wasting away my life attending Him
like one tends on a toddler who
constantly needs its diapers changed?

—The exercise of the sit and stand, five times a day

Poems That Lose

I turn on the news
and there's a rape case being discussed.

I flip the channel
and a crying victim of marital rape
is being interviewed by an uninterested dude.

I don't know if I should celebrate
that finally rape is being discussed out in the open

or

mourn the fact that people still are being raped.

Kind looking folks.
Educated middle-aged men.
School teachers.
Old bosses overdosed on power.
Preachers in the church.
Husbands of pretty girls.
Grandfathers.
Uncles and aunties.

—So many rapists

Dumbbells in a gym never made a man.
Learning to shoot guns never made a man.
Staring contests with friends, undressing
women on the streets never made a man.
There can be no peace in this world until we
teach men to hold books as preciously as they
are taught to hold back their tears.

Mothers, allow your sons to cry.
Fathers, ask your sons to lower their gaze.

—Man up

Let's talk about abuse I said;
and the first few ran off and hid behind the door, unwilling to speak.

Let's talk of the times when we were touched in places we didn't want to be touched;
and there went the next few, running, hiding, terrified to speak.

Let's talk of when someone we knew abused us and got away with it because we never said a word;
and there went the rest of them, only this time screaming in incoherent babbles and a few occasional no(s).

"No we won't talk", says one from behind the wall, trying to hide his face in the shadow of another. "It didn't happen to us," says the girl next to him, also hiding. "You're alone in this, and hence the shame is on you."

"Isn't only that the problem?" I said, "the shame is on me, for sure," my voice trailing off into hopeless silence. "The shame has always been on the one who speaks first, the one who speaks at all."

—The conversation no one wants to have

Shame

noun.

1. the feeling that person should feel
   who first introduced you to this word.

—Dictionary of truth

Poems That Lose

"Men don't cry," exclaims my father, in a stern,
macho voice.
I am 11 years old and there is nothing I know to do
best than run to the corner and weep for hours at our
ancestral pride.
  Brine runs in the blood of men in my family.
Tears dig tunnels and sweat out through their shirts.

I am touching thirty now, and I have seen my father
fight away his life.
He was right. He was so right.
Men don't cry. They pickle their hearts and die.

—*Men don't cry*

I am young but I am getting there. The yellow leaf is going to be upon me, and often I ponder on the discrepancies age brings to the table every time we give it undue weight. Frail and unjust, and all the negative connotations but one: wisdom.

"I have thirty-five more years of experience about life," he says, "I have lived thirty-five years more than you."

"But have you seen more? Have you experienced more?" I ask, "Can't you see that you have lived the same one year thirty-five times over?"

"Age is just a number," he digresses, and I let him move to a new topic. I have nothing more to add anyway, and him, I guess, he has a lot of living to do. But then again, I am young, and soon the yellow leaf will be upon me. I just hope when that happens, I'd have had the courage to have lived.

—Some conversations I have in my head with my father

Poems That Lose

You are a winter thing.
Candescent.
The enemy of all things gloomy.
The death of the color blue.
You are the glow. You are the light. You are *noor*.
They will come looking for you.
They are lost. And they are cold.
What else can you expect?
They will come hunting.
With their spears, and their arrows,
and all things sharp.
Every time the mercury drops
and their own blood is not enough to keep them
warm,
They will come looking.
And at the end of it all,
When the winter is over,
And they are well-fed,
Warm enough to leave,
They will leave.
And you will be left with questions in your head
and an unbearable ache in your heart.
And it will not be wintertime for the world.
The sun will be out for everyone but you.
And your insides will feel cold.
You will be lost.
And it will be your time to go looking for that
warmth.
That *noor*.
In other *winter things*.
In other *candescent* beings.
And you will gather your spears
and sharpen your arrows.
And you will break hearts. *(contd.)*

So many hearts.
And this cycle will continue.
All this is a given.
But what will change everything is
your learning of an important virtue.
The virtue of forgiveness.
And that will be your revolution.

—The revolution of the youth

Poems That Lose

I will embrace you like an apology,
you will swallow me whole like a pill,
and we will build homes out of this;

empty promises for bricks,
a handful of forevers for walls,
and a garden full of cacti called hope
to cut ourselves with when we
feel the urge to be loved.

We will play this drunken stupor
called love like a game and keep winning.
We will trample all the jasmines as we dance,
we will kill all the roses as we bloom,
and our youth will teach us things we wish
we didn't need.

Lover, we will learn how to lose.
Stay.
Until we learn how to lose.

—*Young love*

Akif Kichloo

Love leaves a sour
aftertaste once it's over.
It doesn't end where it's
mutually decided
to have ended.

—The crooked timelines of love

"That's the beauty of childhood:
You have people,
who for some mysterious reason
are ready to die for you.
And you ask me why children
are so happy all the time?
They have love,
to gulp, to eat, to waste.
So much of it."

—*So bloody much of it*

I am not a treasure,
or a work of art,
or an ocean of light.
I know not if I need to close my eyes
or open them in order to see myself.
But what I know is this:
Even the rising sun is a dying star
And all of us deserve to be loved

—*Equally.*

Poems That Lose

That stone they tell you
your heart has turned into?
Tell them,
that's the weight of all your
sufferings.

—Tell them or else they won't know

Akif Kichloo

Hold my hand, I wanted to tell the universe.
Comfort me.

There were rosemary shrubs growing in my garden,
and according to my mother they were going
to bring me luck.
But all of my roses were dying,
Seemed like I had swallowed all the bees.

How could a day like this be lucky?

Hold my hand, I finally mustered up some
courage and asked the universe,

and all the universe ever did
was spit my wishes back at me.

—The day I stopped asking

Poems That Lose

Something hits me
like a violent jab.
I know not if it's love
or loneliness.
There is a buzz in the air
hinting I am not alone,
but this ringing in my ear
tells me otherwise.
Is there someone out there
calling me
into their chaos,
or is it just another
melancholy dream
of romancing death?
There is something urgent
something mournful
about this loneliness— is there not?
Like two lovers kissing for the last time.

—*Loneliness*

Akif Kichloo

There are demons on my shoulders they can't see.
They keep telling me it is nothing.

—Depression

Poems That Lose

O the simplicity
       in the heart
       of this person
       I have become;
I wait well past
       my bed-time
       for monsters
       to come.

—Love me like my demons do

When it first hit me
It was like going from a fairytale
to sitting in a dark room;
scared and confused—
choking on something I knew nothing about,
for reasons I could not comprehend.

One day my therapist compared
it to drowning.

The first question that
popped into my head:

if it were like drowning,
why didn't I flail my arms for decades?
Why calling for help didn't come to me
even as an afterthought?

For years,
doing nothing,
absolutely nothing,
and just trying to get comfortable
with it.

— *That's depression.*

Poems That Lose

If death were a place, then I must be circling it.
This awareness of mortality has pushed me to madness—
that is to say, brought me closer to great things.

From time to time, there rises in me,
like a bursting bubble, an awareness,
a clarity, that the sense of life is in the extremes.
You either live it consumed by its fire,
or spend it resigned to
the mediocrity of the experience (the intermediary stage),
which is just another way of saying,
you either go insane by the very act of living
(circling death like a hawk circles its prey)
or you just sit there waiting for death to come
and take you in handcuffs & shackles;
completely uninterested in what you have to do/say
(Like the life spent).

But then of course, the bubble bursts
and I come back to a much lower orbit,
To the baseline of my living
and become just another face
in the crowd.
(a sheep waiting in line at the slaughterhouse)

—Like the rest of us.

Akif Kichloo

I am in a state of abandon.
Where the world has abandoned me
and I have abandoned the world.
At perfect distance from every
distraction I can offer her
and she can offer me,
we have apologized to each other
and finally decided to move on.
We won't kiss and makeup
but we shall bear no malice as well.
This existence has been like
the perfect day at the beach;
high rising waves, a gentle breeze
and a few sunburns here and there
which have hurt throughout.
Dusk has fallen,
and before we end our truce
like we always do,
Her and I,
we're wise
enough to know when it's time to
bury the hatchet
and call it a night

—*One last time.*

Poems That Lose

She was taught to be humble. Obedience came as an add-on without order or invite. "Be nice," her mother would ask of her, sternly, often threatening her of consequences she wouldn't rather like. Now she points to luck when she achieves something she worked for really hard. She doesn't think much of herself. "I just got lucky," she says, her eyes still firmly fixed at the floor. She dreams, yes, that's her guilty pleasure she tells me in a shy tone. "Girls are home-makers," her father had said a million times already by the time she learnt to speak. "It is scary out there," she parrots her first lovers words, who left a long time ago, but still governs her every scream. "Love," she says, "has been a punitive expedition." More like an afterthought, but somehow she gathers the courage to utter these final words, "If I should ever have a daughter, I won't raise her like this. Come what may, I will make sure she knows she has wings. And I will tell her, I will tell her, it is not a sin if she has it in her to fly."

—*Momma said, "Be nice."*

Akif Kichloo

There are songs in our bodies we don't sing.
There are oceans in our veins we don't taste.
We are trained to live in cages of our names.

—Gender Roles/ Expectations

Poems That Lose

A meaningful conversation.
A deep inculpable thought.
An honest confession of love.
A guilt-free touch.

—Urges I've run from

Akif Kichloo

When I was 7 years old
I carried my world in a satchel.
In it, there were
3 broken pieces of *tinted glass*,
8 *marbles*,
a 2 rupee *note*
and some *candy*.

I am much older now.
But I still carry my world
with me
in a satchel.
In it there are,
3 credit *cards*,
1 faded *picture* of an old lover,
and all my *hurt*.

—*The satchel, the wallet, and the grownup's heart(hurt)*

When I desire a thing
to have,
I blatantly ask for it.
When I crave a body
to hold,
I unashamedly reach out
and touch it.
When I seek a soul
to love,
I quietly look to the sky
and weep.

—Fear of commitment (or just fear)

We fuck like there is someone else
with us in our bed.
Maybe a ghost, maybe a mistress;
Our attention always on orgasms
and never on each other.
We have learnt to disassociate the kissing
from the lips,
we have learnt to to play the *in and out*
routine as a game.
I fuck you thrice every time
you stay the night.
I cum thrice,
You cum thrice;
Never a level playing field
but the score— somehow—
magically equal—
e v e r y-f u c k i n g-t i m e.

—The fucking

Poems That Lose

Each day I say a little less;
Get a little more fluent in
the art of silence.

We are so in love,
O so connected to each other's soul;

Every time I swallow my pride
I can practically see you getting
full of it.
So full of it.

—The shit we sometimes call love

The love we think we understand
can never be the kind we get to have.
What more proof do we need to
understand:

We are most in love when not in love.

The definition of love is elusive;

The ceaseless longing to touch,
the monstrous craving to hold,
the relentless search to find the one,
(for the first time or just for that one time again)
and having no idea how, where, and why.
That's the closest we can ever come

—*To the definite kind of love.*

Poems That Lose

No matter where you come from
or what stories you carry hidden in your back pocket,
Everybody is capable of falling in love.
It's just that, for some it feels like the
greatest feeling in the world; light as a feather,
organic.
And for some—it smells of defeat, of giving up;
the weight of a thousand heartbreaks.
A betrayal to all those moments where you
promised to never let yourself fall into
this trap again.

—Light as a feather, stiff as a board

Akif Kichloo

The journey, from desire to possession,
that's where we are at our best behavior.

In the quest of love, we peak at love.

And right at the culmination of
this intoxicating voyage;
At the opening touch of
the possibility of possession,

without our knowing
the departing begins.

A maddening overlap—
where without warning,
the last few steps towards possession
turn into the first few steps of leaving,
(of abandoning the very thing we craved).

—I love you but I don't know what that means

Poems That Lose

All the trepidations
but here we are,
So happy and so in love.
This is what years of uphill battles
lead you to.
To the edge of the cliff,
smiling like two buffoons,
not knowing what to do next.

Do you know how ridiculous that feeling is:

Finally having what you have dreamt of
all your life and
doing nothing but repeatedly
asking your self:
"what now?"

*—And so it happens, the end of the battle is
where the war begins*

Akif Kichloo

Black Holes And Black Sheep

Life hasn't been very kind of late.
My father says you don't pray enough,
and he says it through my mother.
My mother says *"Call your dad already. It has been six months now."*
But I have been on an auto-pilot kind of
a mood lately.
Letting the wind drift me to the shore.
I have learned that kindness cannot be
expected off everyone
and sometimes all you have to hold is you.
Sometimes the only shoulder you get to cry on
is your own
and no matter how hard you try,
you can't break your neck enough to lean on it.

There are times I walk looking at the sky,
and they tell me you are destined to fall.
If I should have a kid and he walks
looking like that towards the sun,
I would know there might be clouds in his eyes.
But people have better things to do, you know,
than lifting the spirits of a lost soul.
More money to make. Many worries to tend to.

Black holes and black sheep often
look the same from a distance
and who wants to come near any one of
them and get sucked into their abyss?

There are some nights when you
understand why an alcoholic drinks

to the brink of blacking out.
Those nights belong to you. Just you.
No one dares come near you.
"You bring me down," they say.

Scientists have confirmed,
An unhappy friend decreases the likelihood
of you feeling happy by 7 %,
but after the kind of life I have lived,
I will take those odds any day.
A lonely hand needs another and it doesn't
matter what it does to the other hand,
no one deserves to be lonely like that.
Happiness is just a relative thing anyway.
There is no happy without sad.
But there is always lonely without happy
and it is always akin to being sad.
It is not relative anymore.
You don't have to have tasted happiness in
order to feel alone.
You just feel like that sometimes.
But people are too simple to fight the odds.

I have drowned so many times in my own sweat
that the ocean doesn't scare me anymore
and it doesn't matter at this point that
my father never taught me how to swim.

I wish I could tell you the tale of tomorrow
but you have to understand
sometimes just today is enough.
Do you hear me?

And then, I witnessed it,
Defeat turning the ugliest of people into the most empathetic—
So open I could pass through them and become a better man.

"That's the power of failure," said one of them
in a calm, understanding voice.
"It changes something in your very core."
"Gives you that pause, that long needed break to look within."
"And you know what happens when you look within?"
"You drop the act. And you drop all your judgments."

— Isn't this what we need?

Poems That Lose

Wishful Thinking With A Nursery Rhyme

Daddy, dear Daddy
When I grow up,
Don't push me to earn money
and be a bigger man.
Bigger men grow way too tall
(and then with blank faces)
they look down upon us all.

Daddy, dear Daddy,
remember when I was young?
I would wait for my brother
near the school bus.

We would hug, we would kiss,
We would walk home hand in hand.
Remember how happy we looked
sitting on your lap?

But look now Daddy,
My brother—he grew way too tall.
He lives in his castle
away from us all.

And Daddy he thinks of himself the bigger man,
Brings home pay checks as big as the anger on his face.

Daddy, dear Daddy,
where did the smiles go?

(contd.)

Akif Kichloo

We used to be happy
and now all we do is work.

Daddy, dear Daddy,
when I grow up,
I don't want to look down
upon anyone.

Giggles and laughter—
that's all I want.

Daddy, dear Daddy I beg of you,
When I grow up
Don't ask me to earn money
like my brother and you.

And Daddy, dear Daddy
I don't want to be one of those
bigger men.
When I grow up,
I hope you have retired
and we can be poor again.

The Song I Won't Sing

When I die, talk about me.
Make people grow tired of my name.
This body feels older than it should be,
So much it has had to endure.

Long nights, short days, and still counting;
Years turn so slow, and yet I grow old.
The clock keeps sitting at my desk,
One stares at me from the wall.
And I don't know what to tell it,
Other than that it will be here long after I am gone.

Make people tell stories that I made,
Ask if to them I was bad?
You see, I keep trying to do right every morning,
But it gets tiring when the silver night falls.
I have always loved to talk with the moon,
And it answers me in its own special ways.
One day it's big with my delusions,
Then I blink and like everything, it's gone.

I wait for hours to have a worthy conversation,
I was never big for their small talk.
You see, I have had this weird thing with people;
They come only when I am not home.

Tell them, I wrote everyone many letters,
Didn't have the courage to post them all.
The ones who do get to read them,
Please remember my name after I am gone.

Someone once said that a man sees in the world what he carries in his heart.
All I see is sadness.

—*There's no one to blame*

Poems That Lose

My privilege being his son
is that I get to say *he fucked me up
for life*
when it can so easily be the
other way around.

—*Who's the bigger man?*

Akif Kichloo

If you have to love me,
love me in my wilderness,
And if you're ashamed
and want to change me,
I will turn to smoke;
vanish and move on.

I am armed with nothing
but this one truth:

*Where love meets life,
all love disappears.*

I know, I was born out of
a lack of choice,
But I became love the very
moment I knew how to
choose.

And I chose to be love.

—*I am love, I am love, I am love*

Poems That Lose

My feet are stuck to the sky
but I am told that I am an ostrich with
anxiety issues.
So I keep my head inside a hole in the ground.

I fly high (sometimes)
but in hiding.

What keeps me humble?
My lack of fear of dying.

What keeps me grounded?
Knowing what a horrible life it is when
you have your nose up in the sky.

—*An ostrich with anxiety issues*

Akif Kichloo

Tonight seems like
the perfect night for
my resurrection.
For taking the heart out
of the trashcan
and placing it
back into my
chest.

—My night of resurrection

Poems That Lose

It takes both time
and distance
for a piece of paper to age.

Edges—stain,
Page—crumples,
Ink remains the same.

The words breathe their repetitive breaths,
yet their meaning— somehow different;
evolves into something new.

I noticed my mother's hands the other day,
Holding a bone china dish with
custard and jelly, perfectly made.
(Just like she did
when I was a young boy.)

But her hands seemed unfamiliar;
Ebbing skin,
transparent,
you could see her blood through it.

I was never told blood turns bluer as you get old.

What time does to us, distance can limit,
But what then, when we set boundaries
for people who need to be near us?

I have always been heavy,
Could never see my blood through my
thick skin.
Never any transition in my hands to notice;
Time has always played tricks on me, *(contd.)*

Clocks and calendars have always been
confusing for me to understand.

So I cry, still;
My nails grow back so fast.
I chew them away,
But it's like they come back the
very next instant.

I don't want to be my mother's age.
I don't want my mother to be my
mother's age.

—One of the many introductions to the concept of mortality

Poems That Lose

I used to be homesick for
    places I had lived in
    or for *people* I had loved.
Now I have this craving for the *future*
    as if homesick for the *unknown*.

—Homesick

Even though I have,
but my heart has not aged.
It is still as new,
as hopeful
as the "chocolate milk" days.

—*It's the heart that matters*

From rigid, first—you turn soft;
Transform—

from an obstruction
to a scenic road
(open for ways other
than your own).

Then—the fluid state:

your metamorphosis to the liquid form
(limpid but stagnant).

In this stasis,
(paradoxically) you learn to flow.

In obscurity,
In anonymity,
In solitude,
In silence—

this is how you grow.

—How we evolve

If only we could love out of pity,
Or maybe we can.
Who am I to say otherwise?
You see, my pride *exists*,
and it does come in my way
sometime.

I once heard of a town
where fish fell like raindrops
from the sky,
but did it change the purpose of the clouds?
People ate the fish and still expected rain.
This is my metaphor for a love rooted in pity:
It's not love, but it's not anything else as well.

—A love rooted in pity

Some Nights

A stranger to the ways of this world
and a foreigner to myself,
I am a *nowhere man;*

Self-improved but unpresentable.
Not waiting (or at least that's what I tell myself)
for invitations
that will never come.

Where do I dump this
existentialism
(existentialism: what an ugly term).

I am alienated
from world's warm embrace,
aching with solitude's yearning
and my own affection for myself.
(A liberated millennial.
Fallen for the
the rhetoric of
Love yourself,
Love yourself,
Love yourself.)

It's night time
and the thunderstorms are slapping
sense into the trees
and the lightning is burning everything
on its way down to touch the
earth,

(contd.)

And I still can't put the cynic in my head to rest.
(what a shame)

The romantics are tossing and
turning in their graves,
What they see is unbelievable
to their eyes.

Camus and *Sarte*
womanizing in hell as they look down
on me and weep.
(existentialism: what an ugly term, they say after death).

In some nights,
there has to be a balance.

There has to be kissing,
touching,
surrendering and doing away
with the questions in our heads.

In some nights,
there has to be
makings
then— in between of makings,
and then again— more makings of love.

Poems That Lose

I am engulfed in you
/with you,
but this neither brings sorrow
nor joy to my living.
Changes nothing on this day.

I am efficiently distanced;

Neither falling
nor rising in love.

As if stuck
in a futile catastrophe.

*—The fabricated mourning and the factitious
ecstasy of a one sided love*

The day I had my first
heartbreak as a kid,
I was watching the sun set
in my back yard
with a young boy from my class
who was completely
indifferent to
the setting of the sun.
Good riddance, he said,
like a metaphor to the burning
in my chest,
and simply got up
and walked off.

I wish it could still be the same.
Life becomes complicated
when we grow old.
We assign meaning to things
before setting them on fire.

—*The simplicity of the good ol' days*

The Motion Of Death And The Inertia Of Life

Sometimes we do the kind of things we do out of a quiet desperation. Sometimes our hearts point to ways that are not in the right direction. And there is no tonic left in our gin to keep us light. There is no air under our sails to keep us moving. And the only promise that no one seems to be breaking is the promise of the earth-sized holes under our boats (to make sure we drown).

In those days, the reality compounds us. So what do we do but let ourselves fall apart with lightening silence? Of course, the thunder is never heard. There is nothing left inside us to make that sound. (Only poetic good-bye letters and romantic ideas for suicide notes.)

But we live on. (Even when the motion of death feels more appealing than the stagnation of life.) No matter how paramount the inertia is on such days, we breathe and hope for better outcomes. Suitable results. Preferable futures.

But, not all of us. Some of us do succumb completely to our misfortunes. Some of us do strike in one swift motion— a strike to end it all. The trouble, still, is not in our choice, but in our very lack of it. Whatever we choose or don't get to choose, I hope we find a peaceful place to rest our head one starry night. And whatever we do or don't do, I pray the light returns to us the next morning forever more. Because if there is

(contd.)

one thing I have learnt about life, it is this:
If only we'd live long enough, life itself does in the long run teach us how to live it.

And at the end of the day, no matter how well or miserably we think we have lived, we have lived a brilliant life. *Each and every one of us.*

Poems That Lose

Go home to your suffering.
Tend to it as you would a lover—
only if they were there.
Scratch around the wound and it's
okay if you make it bleed.

Before the morning shows up
with its dressing, and its medicine,
and all its unwanted remedies—

Draw the curtains and allow yourself to
cry alone in the dark tonight.

—Go home to your suffering

Say yes!

> To the voices.
> To the noises.
> To the silence.
> To the adventure.
>
> Say yes.
>
> Say yes more often
> and see where you go.
>
> —*Say yes*

Poems That Lose

Some days are for falling in love with people, some days for cities, and some for your time in solitude.

—*Know what day is for what*

The ones—
waiting for a terminal diagnosis
to begin life,

I say this:

The lingering pain inside you
has been there for decades
and is in no hurry to leave.

We were born mortals,
to die
and take nothing with us.

What other terminal illness
is there to wait for?

If you want to liberate your self,
annihilate your self.
Today.

—*Rumi was right*

Poems That Lose

There is no easier way to let go.
Hold onto this grief dearly until
it lets go of you.

—The end

Akif Kichloo

About the Author

Akif Kichloo is a poet, doctor, musician, photographer, and an artist, who currently lives where-ever he can find a kind smile. A graduate of JU, Akif holds a bachelor's degree in medicine and surgery. When he is not pursuing artistic excellence he is either busy looking after his patients or doing clinical research work in the field of anesthesiology.

Akif Kichloo started writing at an early age, having contributed for publications like The Huffington Post and The Wire, he continues to write for various newspapers and magazines internationally. In addition, he was invited to speak at the prestigious TEDx stage at Christ University to present his talk Follow Your Confusion.

Amidst the uncertainties of this amazing, magical, horrible, beautiful life, as he puts it, Akif Kichloo writes on various subjects, posting a couple of poems weekly to his social media pages with a huge following of avid readers and poetry lovers from all over the world.

akifkichloo.com
akifkichloobooks.com
Instagram: @akifkichloo
Twitter: @akifkichloo
Facebook: facebook.com/akifkichloo
Pinterest: pinterest.com/akifkichloo
Tumblr: akifkichloo.com

Akif Kichloo

Poems That Lose

Another book of poems by Akif Kichloo:

The Feeling May Remain

(Available everywhere books and eBooks are sold.)

Akif Kichloo

www.ingramcontent.com/pod-product-compliance
Lightning Source LLC
Chambersburg PA
CBHW020621300426
44113CB00007B/729